Let's Count to
100!

Masayuki Sebe

Kids Can Press

There are 100 mice!
Count them all, starting with the brown ones.

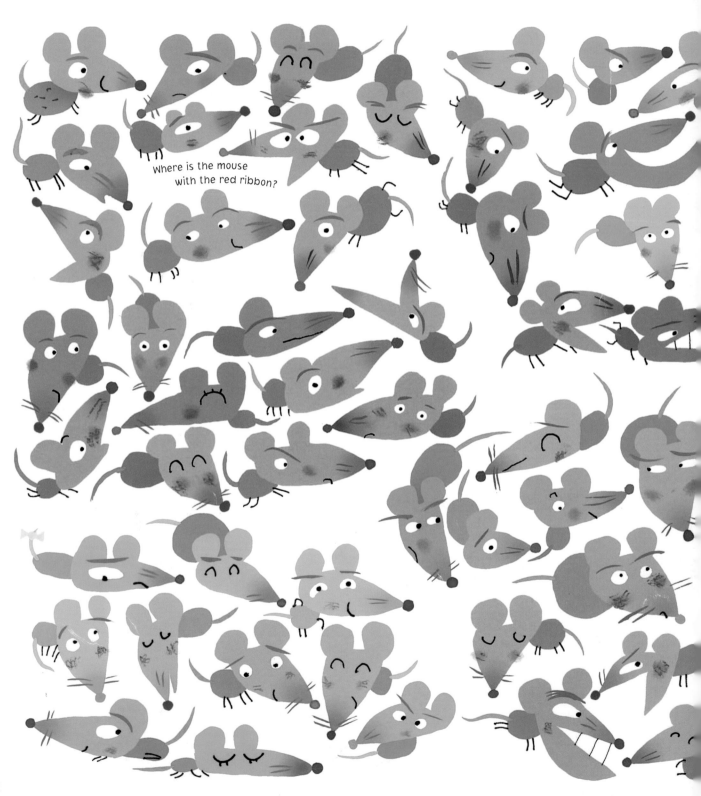

Where is the mouse with the red ribbon?

2

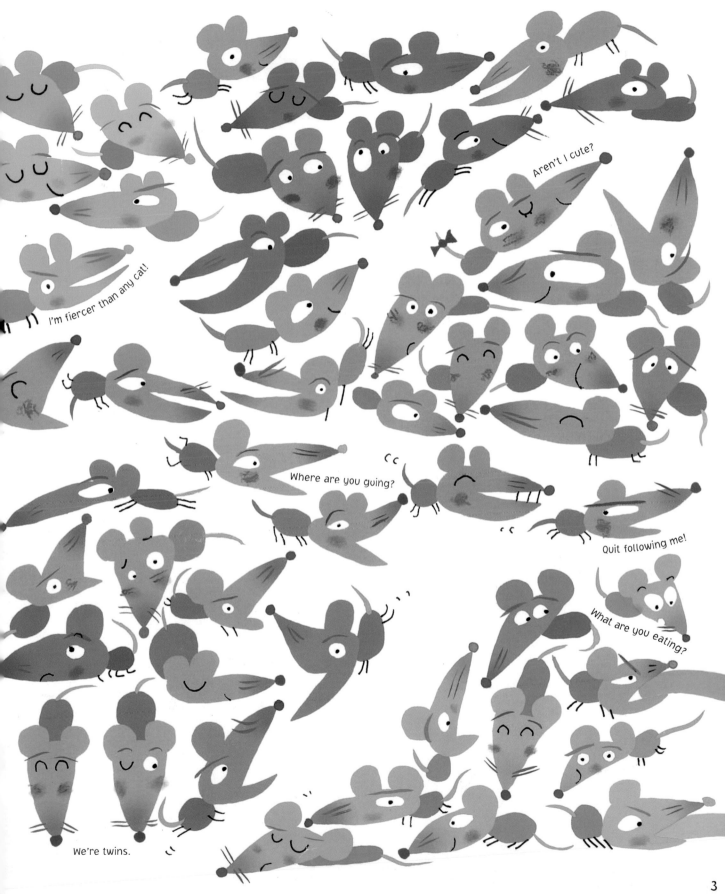

3

There are **100** cats!
How many have striped tails?

Please don't pull my whiskers.

Gotcha!

Hee! That tickles!

How many cats
are in my family?

Who
are you?

Have you seen
the ladybug?

5

There are **100** moles.

What's that?

I don't want to know!

You stink!

Pee-ew!

Ahh! I feel much better.

I'm digging.

Careful!

6

How many are snuggled up with a frog?

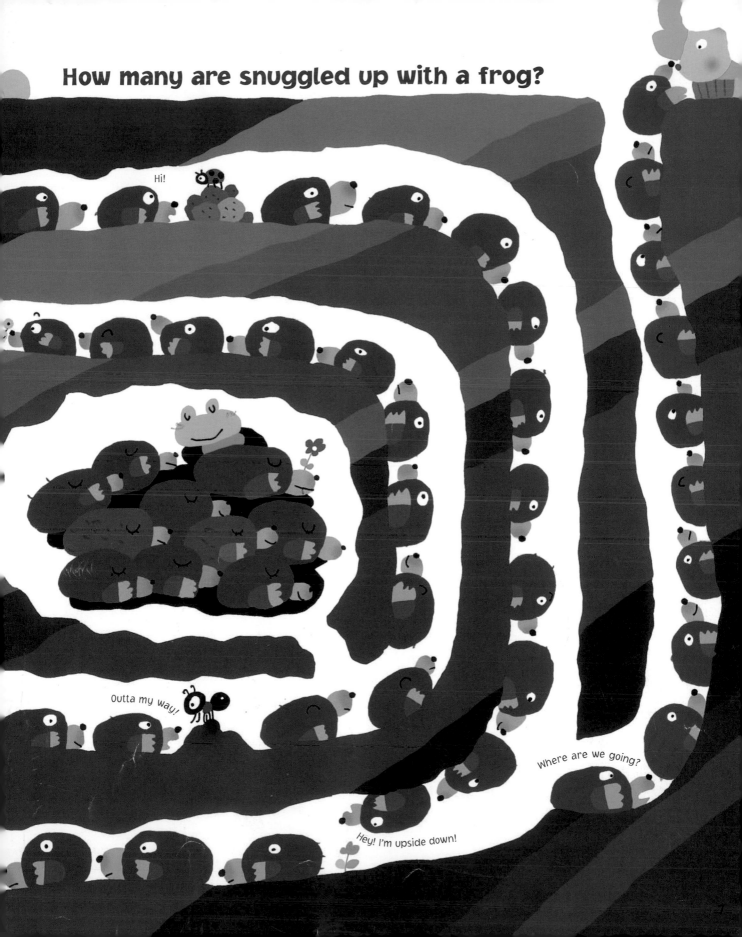

There are **100** sheep ...

Wait for me!

Nice day, isn't it?

Oh!

Hi!

Hello!

How's the grass today?

8

and **1 rabbit!** (Do you see him?)

There are **100** birds.

You look tasty!

Eep!

May I have one, please?

That's one each.

Who's a good chick?

Cheep!

Cheep!

10

Are there enough berries for everyone?

Yum!

I like being upside down.

Got it!

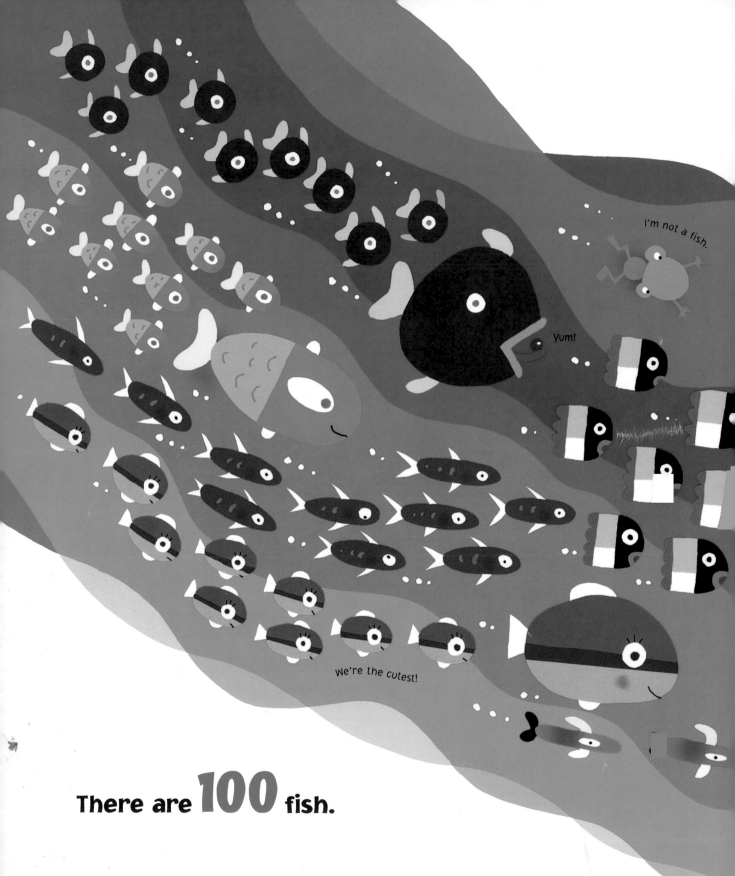

There are **100** fish.

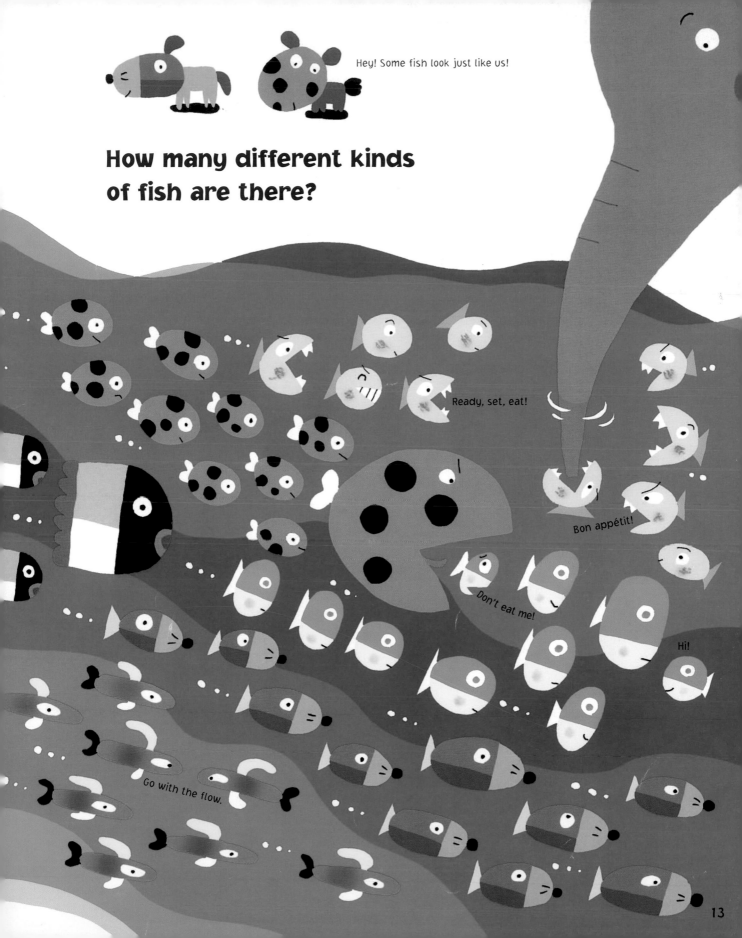

There are **100** elephants!

I need to cool off.

That hurt!

How many elephants are sleeping?

How many elephants are smiling?

I'm lost.

Ready, set, count!

That looks tasty!

There are **100** kids!

Count them all.

There are 100 ants!

How many are carrying candy?

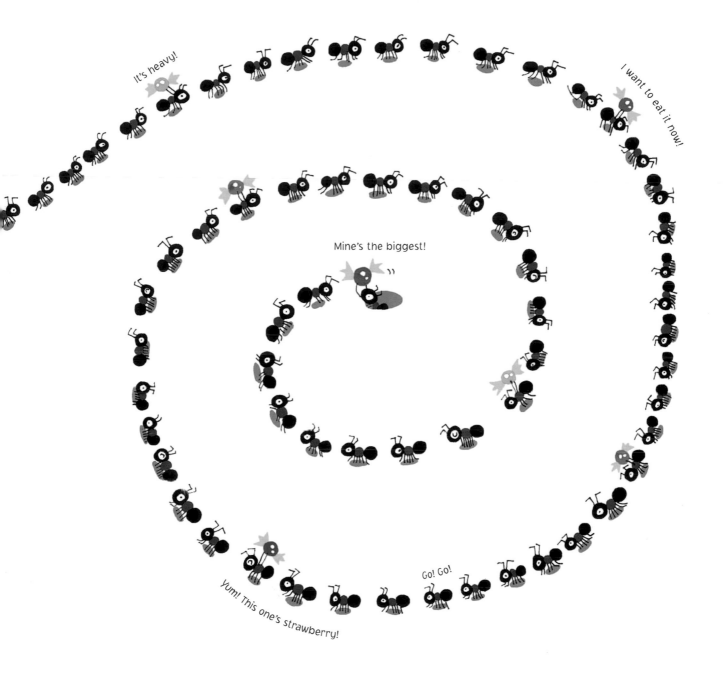

I want a carrot.

Where is the mouse?

Maybe I should play outside.

20

There are **100** cars and trucks!

Beep! Beep!

Woop-woop!

Wee-oo! Wee-oo!

I like watermelon.

And **100** houses!

There are **10** mice, **10** cats, **10** moles, **10** sheep, **10** birds, **10** fish, **10** elephants, **10** kids, **10** ants and **10** houses.

That makes **100** in all!

Tweet! Tweet!

What?

Meow!

Yikes — a cat!

Go! Go! Go!

23

Did you see ...

the mouse with the
yellow bow?
(pages 2–3)

this cat?
(pages 4–5)

the farting mole?
(pages 6–7)

the snowman?
(pages 8–9)

this bird?
(pages 10–11)

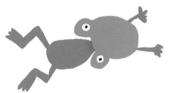

this frog?
(pages 12–13)

the elephant
holding a pineapple?
(pages 14–15)

who was wearing
this hat?
(pages 16–17)

the girl with a
strawberry on her head?
(pages 16–17)

the boy cuddling this
cat?
(pages 16–17)

this sleeping ant?
(pages 18–19)

the mouse's house?
(pages 20–21)

this house?
(pages 20–21)

this truck?
(pages 20–21)

Originally published in Japanese under the title *Kazoetegoran Zembu de 100*
by Kasei-sha Publishing Co., Ltd.
English translation rights arranged through Japan Foreign-Rights Centre

Kids Can Press acknowledges the financial support of the Government of Ontario, through the Ontario Media Development Corporation's Ontario Book Initiative; the Ontario Arts Council; the Canada Council for the Arts; and the Government of Canada, through the BPIDP, for our publishing activity.

Published in Canada by
Kids Can Press Ltd.
25 Dockside Drive
Toronto, ON M5A 0B5

Published in the U.S. by
Kids Can Press Ltd.
2250 Military Road
Tonawanda, NY 14150

www.kidscanpress.com

English edition edited by Yvette Ghione

This book is smyth sewn casebound.
Manufactured in Tseung Kwan O, NT Hong Kong, China, in 3/2011 by Paramount Printing Co. Ltd.

CM 11 0 9 8 7 6 5 4 3 2 1

Library and Archives Canada Cataloguing in Publication

Sebe, Masayuki, 1953–
    Let's count to 100! / written and illustrated by Masayuki Sebe.

Translation of: Kazoetegoran zembu de 100.
ISBN 978-1-55453-661-0

1. Counting — Juvenile literature. 2. Picture books for children. I. Title.

QA113.S44 2011   j513.2'11   C2011-900084-9